# The Scopes Trial

Withdrawn

**CORNERSTONES OF FREEDOM**
SECOND SERIES

Renee Graves

**Children's Press®**
A Division of Scholastic Inc.
New York • Toronto • London • Auckland • Sydney
Mexico City • New Delhi • Hong Kong
Danbury, Connecticut

Photographs © 2003: AP/Wide World Photos: 17, 20, 22, 25, 31, 44 top right, 45 top; Brown Brothers: cover top, 4, 5, 6, 7, 12, 15, 24, 26, 32, 44 top left, 45 bottom right; Bryan College Archives: 37 (NewYork Journal), 3, 13, 14, 23, 27, 41, 45 left, 45 top right; Corbis Images: cover bottom, 18, 21, 29, 33 (Bettmann), 16, 35 (Underwood & Underwood); Hulton|Archive/Getty Images: 8, 9, 44 bottom; Photofest: 30; Superstock, Inc./Culver Pictures Inc.: 10; University of Tennessee, Knoxville/The Special Collections Library: 38.

Library of Congress Cataloging-in-Publication Data
Graves, Renee.
   The Scopes trial / Renee Graves.
      p. cm. — (Cornerstones of freedom. Second series)
   Summary: A description of the historic 1925 trial in which a Tennessee high school biology teacher was accused of violating state law by teaching Darwin's theory of evolution.
   Includes bibliographical references and index.
      ISBN 0-516-24221-0
      1. Scopes, John Thomas—Trials, litigation, etc.—Juvenile literature. 2. Evolution—Study and teaching—Law and legislation—Tennessee—Juvenile literature. [1. Scopes, John Thomas—Trials, litigation, etc. 2. Evolution—Study and teaching—Law and legislation.] I. Title. II. Series.
KF224.S3G73 2003
345.73'0288—dc21

                                        2003005618

1 2 3 4 5 6 7 8 9 10 R 12 11 10 09 08 07 06 05 04 03

ON JULY 10, 1925, THE SMALL Tennessee town of Dayton was overflowing with people. All of the hotel rooms were filled for several miles around. The city streets were busy and noisy, even though the city was in the middle of a horrible heat wave. People crowded the hot dog stands and souvenir counters that had recently been built, and there was an air of excitement as people gossiped and ate ice cream cones while strolling up and down the street. Evangelists stood on street corners, holding up their Bibles and preaching in loud voices to anyone who would stop and listen.

★ ★ ★ ★

Clarence Darrow speaks to a packed courtroom in Dayton, Tennessee, during the so-called Scopes Monkey Trial. The trial pitted two of the country's most famous speakers—Darrow and William Jennings Bryan—against each other as opposing attorneys.

Large, colorful signs and banners hung across the front of every shop. Chimpanzees performed in a sideshow on Main Street, and in the city's main drugstore, a monkey dressed up in a little suit and hat perched on a counter and drank bottles of Coke, to the delight of spectators of all ages. What was going on in Dayton on that hot summer day? Was it a religious revival, or possibly the circus? Was it the county fair? No, it was the first day of the "Scopes Trial," a court case that is possibly one of the most important trials ever to be held in America.

4

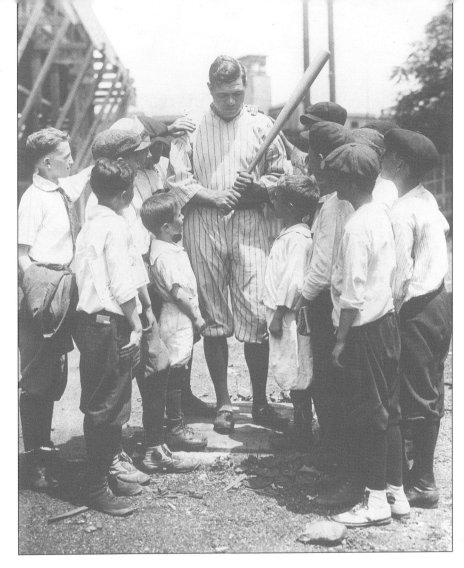

Babe Ruth of the New York Yankees was America's greatest athletic hero during the "Roaring Twenties," a decade when everything, even the national pastime, seemed to be changing in ways that left many people bewildered. Before the slugging Ruth, home runs were a rarity in baseball, but one season Ruth hit more homers than any other team in the American League.

The United States was going through a lot of major changes at the time of the Scopes Trial. World War I had just ended, and the men who returned home from the European battlegrounds brought foreign ideas and new perspectives back home with them. New theories about all aspects of culture were being widely discussed for the first time in America. In addition to this, many people felt that now that the war was over, it was time for America to relax. Many Americans were eager to celebrate and embrace a liberal, more carefree lifestyle.

However, there were also those who thought that Americans were becoming too wild and that the country was becoming immoral. Many people who felt this way began joining together to urge people to return to more conservative

The 1920s were a time of great change in American society. One of the biggest changes was brought about by the ratification of the 18th Amendment, in 1920, which led to Prohibition—a time when the manufacture and sale of alcoholic beverages was illegal in the United States. Here, a federal government "revenue man" pours out some confiscated liquor.

ways of thinking. "Christian fundamentalism" became one of the more popular movements among people who were worried about the way the country was changing. The Christian fundamentalists believed that the problems in the country would be solved if Americans returned to a more strict interpretation of the Bible. Fundamentalist preachers traveled across America and gathered huge followings, especially in the rural South.

One of the new ideas that upset the fundamentalists was a theory called evolution. Evolution is a scientific theory that tries to help explain how organisms—plants, animals, and even humans—developed on the earth. The idea of evolution was fairly new in the 1920s. In 1859, an English scientist named Charles Darwin wrote *The Origin of Species*, one of the first books about evolution. By the 1920s, the theories in his book were becoming widely accepted by other scientists.

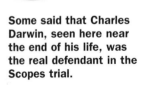

Some said that Charles Darwin, seen here near the end of his life, was the real defendant in the Scopes trial.

The fundamentalists were against the idea of evolution because it suggests that animals evolved, or changed, from being one thing into being something else. Instead, the fundamentalists believe that less than about six thousand years ago, God created each animal exactly as they are now. This belief is called

### NATURAL SELECTION

In his book, Darwin said that all plants and animals slowly evolve, or change, over a very long period of time. If a plant or an animal changes in a way that makes it stronger, then that plant or animal has a better chance at survival. Darwin called this process of change "natural selection," because it described how "nature" would select the animals that were the strongest. This idea is also known as "survival of the fittest," although Darwin himself did not use that term.

Jazz was another new form of entertainment that delighted and disturbed Americans in the 1920s. Many people found the new music sinful, in part because of its association with African-American culture. This is King Oliver's Creole Jazz Band, with the immortal Louis Armstrong (standing, center) on trumpet.

"creationism," and it is based on the Biblical story of creation that can be found in the Book of Genesis.

Many fundamentalists disagree most with the theory as it applies to human evolution. Fundamentalists believe that God placed both man and woman, fully formed, on the earth. However, many evolutionists believe that man may have evolved instead from its closest genetic relative—the monkey family. They suggest that about five million years ago, humans evolved from a branch of primates that included chimpanzees.

# THE BUTLER ACT

Tension between liberal Americans and conservative Americans was running high by 1925, and the country was becoming more and more divided. Fundamentalist leaders began to preach heavily against ideas that they believed were contrary to the teachings of the Bible. One of the people who heard the fundamentalist arguments against evolution was a Tennessee politician named John Butler.

As Butler would later explain to a reporter at the Scopes trial, he had heard a traveling speaker preach against evolution at his church. The visiting preacher had told a story about three young women who went away to college and were taught evolution. The preacher said that because they learned evolution, they stopped believing in God. Butler added that he was worried about the same thing happening to his own three teen-aged boys, or to his neighbor's children.

Butler reasoned that since the public schools were funded by tax money from the people, then the people should have some say in what was taught. If the people didn't want their children learning about evolution, then he believed that they had a right to say so. He wrote a law that said it should be illegal for any teacher in a public school

This 1860s British cartoon demonstrates the ridicule met with by Darwin for proposing his theory of evolution. Opponents feared that Darwin was literally trying to make a monkey of human beings.

## WHAT'S IN A NAME

Because the theory of human evolution states that humans evolved from monkeys, people gave the Scopes Trial the nickname of "the Scopes Monkey Trial." Many people still refer to the trial by that name today.

## WHAT TO TEACH

Even though the Butler Act passed into law, few people thought that it would ever be enforced. One reason that many people didn't take the law very seriously was because the high school biology textbook that was approved by the state of Tennessee was an evolutionary textbook. Few people believed that the state would actually bring a teacher to court for teaching from the state-appointed textbook.

"to teach any theory that denies the story of the divine creation of man as taught in the Bible, and to teach instead that man descended from a lower order of animals." Many people understood this to mean that it would be against the law to teach evolution in Tennessee public schools. This law passed the Tennessee legislature in March of 1925 and was named the Butler Act, after its author.

Even though some people didn't take the new law very seriously, one group in New York City did. This group was

Although Americans in the 1920s flocked by the thousands to watch "talking" movies, others saw this new entertainment phenomenon as yet another sign that their country was changing beyond recognition.

the American Civil Liberties Union (or ACLU, for short). The ACLU was a new organization in 1925. Its purpose was to protect the rights that Americans are granted in the constitution. The ACLU decided that the Butler Act was unconstitutional because it violated the First Amendment to the Constitution. This Amendment guarantees that there should be a separation of church and state. The ACLU pointed out that the Butler Act was based on fundamentalist religious beliefs. They said that writing a law that is based on religious beliefs violated the constitutional separation of church and state.

The ACLU decided to challenge the law in court in the hope that they could get the law repealed. Before they could bring the law to trial, however, they had to find someone willing to go to court as a defendant. The ACLU placed an ad in all of the major Tennessee newspapers. It said, "We are looking for a Tennessee teacher who is willing to accept our services in testing this law in the courts. Our lawyers think a friendly test case can be arranged without costing a teacher his or her job . . . All we need now is a willing client."

## JOHN SCOPES— THE "WILLING CLIENT"

John Scopes was only 24 years old when he agreed to be the defendant in what would soon be called "the Greatest Trial of the Century." He was a very young looking man with red hair and horn-rimmed glasses. People described him as being shy, friendly, and modest, and said that he was very

**Defendant John Scopes stands before the judge.**

well liked by his students. He had only been teaching for nine months and was the high school football coach. He also taught physics and math. Evolution was a topic that was taught in biology, not in any of the classes that Scopes was hired to teach. However, Scopes had been a substitute for a while when the regular biology teacher was away.

Although Scopes agreed to be the defendant in the case, he didn't come up with the idea himself. A man named George Rappalyea asked Scopes to volunteer. In fact, many people have said that there never could have been a "Scopes Trial" without Rappalyea.

George Rappalyea was the manager of Cumberland Coal and Iron, which had once been a very profitable mining company. Rappalyea's company had been the major source

An opponent of religious fundamentalism, George Rappalyea approached both the American Civil Liberties Union (ACLU) and John Scopes about making a test case of Tennessee's anti-evolution law.

13

of employment for people in Dayton for years. By 1913, however, most of the coal had been mined out of the vein and Cumberland Coal and Iron was bankrupt. As people left Dayton to find work in other cities, Dayton's population dropped from 3,000 to 1,800. The town was beginning to struggle economically.

After George Rappalyea saw the ACLU advertisement in the newspaper, he came up with a plan that he knew would bring business to Dayton. Any court battle about evolution was sure to attract national attention. He showed the ACLU ad to Fred Robinson, the school board president and the

Robinson's Drug Store in Dayton was proud to claim the distinction of being the place where the Scopes trial had been planned.

14

H. L. Mencken was the country's best-known newspaper columnist and political commentator at the time of the Scopes trial. Mencken believed that "religion, generally speaking, has been a curse to mankind." It was thus no surprise when his columns on the trial brutally ridiculed the anti-evolutionists as buffoons, quacks, and even primates.

## BAD PUBLICITY?

By the time the trial was over, the town of Dayton had received a lot of publicity. Unfortunately, it might not have been the kind of publicity that Rappalyea and Robinson had hoped for. More than 200 journalists from across the nation (and around the world) came to Dayton to cover the trial. Most of the journalists were from larger cities, however, and they didn't fit in very well in small-town Dayton. While nearly all of the citizens of Dayton were fundamentalists who sided with the prosecution, most of the journalists were liberals who sided with the defense. This caused many journalists to portray Dayton in a negative light. In fact, H.L. Mencken, the most famous journalist in America at the time, called the people of Dayton "yokels," "primates," "morons," "half-wits," and "hillbillies" in his news reports. Mencken's reports for his newspaper, the *Baltimore Sun*, were widely read and believed by the rest of America.

owner of Robinson's Drug Store, Dayton's central meeting place. Robinson agreed that the trial might bring tourist dollars to the town.

John Scopes was playing tennis with some friends when Rappalyea and Robinson sent word that they wanted to meet with him at Robinson's Drug Store. When he arrived, Rappalyea asked Scopes if he had been teaching the biology students the lessons from the approved biology textbook.

(From left) George Rappalyea, school superintendent Walter White, Fred Robinson, and John Scopes recreate the famous meeting at which they first discussed having Scopes get himself arrested for teaching evolution.

Scopes said that he had, while he was substituting in the class. Rappalyea pointed out that the text contained material on evolution. Scopes agreed that it did. "Then you've been violating the law," Rappalyea told him. "Would you be willing to stand for a test case?" he asked. Scopes was hesitant at first, but then agreed to go along with the plan. Rappalyea contacted the ACLU to tell them that he had their defendant, and Scopes was arrested by the town constable and released until the trial began. The stage was set for one of the most influential trials of the century.

## BRYAN AND DARROW—THE "STARS" OF THE SHOW

Although the trial was named after John Scopes, he was certainly not the center of the public's interest. In fact, he didn't even testify at his own trial. America was far more curious about the real "stars" of the show—William Jennings Bryan and Clarence Darrow.

William Jennings Bryan was 65 years old when he volunteered to be a lawyer for the prosecution in the Scopes trial. He had already had a long and distinguished career as a politician, journalist, and lawyer. He had been a congressman

The world-famous William Jennings Bryan (left) was joined as prosecuting attorney in the Scopes case by his son, William Jennings Bryan, Jr. (right).

A three-time nominee for president of the United States, Bryan was known as the "Great Commoner" for his defense of the interests of farmers and the rural working class. He was most famous for his 1896 "Cross of Gold" speech, which is the subject of this cartoon.

for the state of Nebraska and had run for president three times as a candidate for the Democratic Party. He had also served as a secretary of state for President Woodrow Wilson. Politically, Bryan was a "progressive," or someone who believed strongly in equality and in social and political reform. He was called "the Great Commoner" because he said that he was "in favor of everything that was for the good of the common man." Because of this, most of rural America loved Bryan.

By 1921, however, Bryan had given up his career in politics in order to concentrate on fighting the theory of evolution. As a fundamentalist Christian, Bryan was convinced that Darwin's theory (which he referred to as "ape-ism") was responsible for many of the problems in the world.

Bryan was not the only lawyer for the prosecution, however. He was joined by A.T. Stewart, the attorney general for eastern Tennessee; Ben McKenzie, the former attorney general for eastern Tennessee; William Jennings Bryan, Jr., Bryan's son, and Herbert and Sue Hicks, a local husband and wife team of attorneys.

Clarence Darrow was not the only lawyer for the defense either, although, much like Bryan, he was the one who got the most publicity. Joining Darrow was Arthur Garfield Hayes (who was technically in charge of the defense team); Dudley Field Malone, who was famous as a divorce lawyer;

**THE WEAKEST LINK**

William Jennings Bryan was especially concerned about the idea of "survival of the fittest." Bryan was afraid that people could use this idea to argue that people who were weak weren't important to society. "The Darwinian theory represents man as reaching his present perfection by the operation of the law of hate," he said. "Evolution is the merciless law by which the strong crowd out and kill off the weak."

Darrow (right) was joined in the defense of Scopes by two other nationally known attorneys, Dudley Field Malone (left) and Dr. John K. Neal (center).

and John Randolph Neal, a local lawyer. However, it was clear to the trial's audience that Darrow was the "star."

Clarence Darrow was nearly 70 years old when he volunteered to defend John Scopes. He was possibly the most famous lawyer in America at the time, and was best known for defending labor leaders and radicals, as well as high-profile murderers. Scopes was the only client that Darrow ever volunteered to represent for free, because, as he said, he "really wanted to take part in it."

Darrow, like Bryan, had been interested in politics at one time, and had even supported Bryan's first presidential campaign. He did not support Bryan's fundamentalist beliefs, however. Darrow was an agnostic, and was deeply disturbed by the popularity of the fundamentalist movement. He believed that the fundamentalists were trying to write laws that were based on their religious beliefs without considering the beliefs of other people—people who might not agree with them. He was also a fan of Darwin, and said that he "had read all of Darwin's books as fast as they were published." Darrow had been trying to challenge Bryan to a public debate about science and religion for years, but had never been successful in arranging the meeting. At the Scopes trial, Darrow finally got the chance that he had been waiting for.

## A LAST HURRAH

The Scopes trial would be the last great trial for both Bryan and Darrow. William Jennings Bryan, who suffered from severe diabetes, died in his sleep five days after the trial ended. Clarence Darrow died in Chicago thirteen years later, at the age of 80.

Clarence Darrow (center) with Nathan Leopold (left) and Richard Loeb (right). Leopold and Loeb were defendants in one of Darrow's most famous cases before the Scopes trial. Although the two were convicted of the kidnapping and "thrill-killing" of a fourteen-year-old boy, Darrow succeeded in saving them from the electric chair.

**Judge John Raulston posed for a photograph outside a Dayton hotel during a pause in the Scopes trial. Before the trial, Raulston was known as a "popular local attorney of no special competence."**

# THE TRIAL BEGINS

By the time Bryan and Darrow arrived in Dayton, it looked as though a circus had come to town. Nearly a thousand people jammed into the Rhea County Courthouse on the first day of the trial—about double the amount that the courthouse could easily seat. The judge for the trial was a large man named John Raulston who had already publicly declared that he was a conservative Christian. After a jury of twelve men was selected (eleven of whom were also regular churchgoers), the trial was adjourned for the weekend.

On July 13, the trial arguments finally began. Although Darrow was hired to defend John Scopes, the goal of the defense team was not really to get Scopes declared "not guilty." The defense admitted that Scopes had taught evolution. Instead, Darrow hoped to get Judge Raulston to declare the Butler Act unconstitutional, which meant that the indictment against Scopes would be "quashed," or declared to be no good. After all, if a law is declared to be unconstitutional, then a person can't be arrested for breaking it. On the first day of argument, Darrow asked Judge Raulston to declare the Butler Act to be unconstitutional. Raulston refused.

Darrow was forced to go to his second plan. He had gathered scientific witnesses who were going to testify about evolution. He also had experts on religion who were going to testify that many people didn't believe that evolution and religion contradicted one another. Darrow was hoping that the trial would become a science lesson for the whole world,

Spectators at the Scopes trial milling about in downtown Dayton. Some of those who planned the Scopes trial hoped that it would bring publicity, visitors, and money to Dayton.

## MEDIA CIRCUS

A reporter named Marcet Haldeman-Julius described the scene on the first day of the trial: "Evangelists' shouts mingled with those of vendors . . . The entire courthouse yard literally was given over to preachers who peddled their creeds as if they were so many barbecue sandwiches . . . On the second floor of the old brick courthouse, one entered a wide, spacious freshly painted courtroom with a normal seating capacity of about four or five hundred. I felt as if I had stepped into pandemonium. Men and women jostled with each other; a battalion of newspaper photographers and movie men literally wrestled for advantageous positions; just outside the bar enclosure, muffled telegraph instruments ticked and reporters for the big (newspapers) sat dripping with sweat, writing in pencil or on typewriters as if for their very lives; people stood in aisles and three deep against the back walls; in spite of the big open windows, the air was stifling . . ."

because all of the reporters who were covering the trial would report on what his experts said.

However, Darrow also realized that he did not stand a very good chance of changing Judge Raulston's mind about the Butler Act being unconstitutional. The defense team decided that in the end they needed to allow Scopes to lose the case so that they could appeal the decision to the state supreme court.

They believed that they would have a better chance of getting the Tennessee Supreme Court to rule that the Butler Act was unconstitutional.

Bryan saw the case differently than Darrow did. He didn't agree that the Scopes Trial should be about whether or not the law was constitutional. Instead, he pointed out that the trial was supposed to be about whether or not Scopes had broken the law. Since Scopes himself admitted that he had, Bryan believed that he should be found guilty and fined. Bryan was prepared, however, to defend the Butler Act in court because he understood that Darrow would attack the

**Readers check out anti-evolutionary books and pamphlets at a sidewalk display set up by a local anti-evolution organization in Dayton. T. T. Martin was a crusading evangelist who strongly opposed the teaching of evolution.**

From his desk in the Dayton courthouse, Judge John Raulston reads his decision in the Scopes trial to reporters and onlookers.

law. Bryan looked forward to having another opportunity to publicly argue against teaching evolution.

Since Bryan and his prosecution team were concentrating on whether or not Scopes broke the law, their turn presenting their case was over very quickly. They only called a few witnesses, all of whom testified that Scopes had taught evolution when he substituted in the biology class. After the jury heard these witnesses, the prosecution rested. It was the defense's turn.

The jury in the Scopes trial takes a break outside the courthouse. All the members of the jury were white males. Tennessee law at the time prohibited African Americans or women from serving on a jury.

# DARROW'S SCIENCE LESSON

The defense's first witness was a scientist who was supposed to explain the theory of evolution. However, Bryan objected to Darrow's witness. He pointed out that the trial was supposed to be about whether or not Scopes broke the law, not about evolution. Judge Raulston decided that he wanted to hear what the defense witness had to say before he ruled on whether or not he would allow the witness to speak to the jurors. The jurors were asked to leave, and Darrow's witness testified. After Judge Raulston heard the witness, he dismissed the court for the day.

However, when the trial began again, Judge Raulston ruled that none of the testimony from any of Darrow's expert witnesses would be admitted. The jury was not allowed to hear any of the scientific evidence for evolution. This made Darrow very angry. He accused the judge of being biased for the prosecution. Judge Raulston was insulted by his accusation, and he found Darrow to be in contempt of court. This serious charge could have earned Darrow a fine or even jail

John Scopes (left) and George Rappalyea (right) flank attorney John Neal as they make their way to court beneath a huge banner urging, READ YOUR BIBLE.

time. However, Darrow apologized to Judge Raulston and the contempt charge was dropped.

On the next day of court, some of the things that Darrow's scientific and religious experts had prepared to say in the trial were read aloud. This was so that their statements could be reviewed if the case was appealed to the state supreme court. However, since Judge Raulston had decided that the expert's testimony couldn't be used in the current trial, the experts themselves weren't allowed to personally speak.

Darrow had only partially succeeded in what he had set out to do. Although his experts hadn't been allowed to give their full testimony, parts of their testimony were heard when they were read aloud in court. Journalists from all over the world had indeed reported on what was read. This meant that Darrow had succeeded in giving the world a free science lesson. However, he was frustrated because it was a smaller lesson than he had wanted. He was also frustrated that he had not been able to debate Bryan yet, as he had hoped. Darrow decided to try something different—something that would involve Bryan directly. Darrow was about to do something that had never been done before in an American court.

## THE GREAT DEBATE

On the following Monday, the crowd arrived believing it would be hearing the closing statements from the lawyers. After all, Bryan and the prosecution had already made their case when they pointed out that Scopes had confessed,

* * * *

A huge crowd gathers outside the Dayton courthouse for the Scopes trial. Although the trial did bring much attention to the little Tennessee town, much of the publicity was negative.

which meant that they were finished. Darrow and the defense had also seemed to run out of things to say, since the judge ruled that their witnesses weren't allowed to testify. It didn't look like there could possibly be anything else

Melvyn Douglas (standing, left), as a Darrow-like attorney, argues his point in a 1950s Broadway production of *Inherit the Wind*, the popular play based on the Scopes trial. *Inherit the Wind* was a popular success in stage, film, and television versions.

## FICTION FROM FACT

The debate between the defense lawyer and the prosecution lawyer is portrayed dramatically in a movie called *Inherit the Wind*, which was loosely based on the Scopes trial. The movie, which was made in 1960, did not claim to show the Scopes trial exactly as it happened, however. The names of all of the characters from the trial were changed for the movie, and several important facts were changed as well.

left, except for the closing statements. Even so, a huge crowd assembled. The closing speeches from the two greatest speechmakers in America would be something to hear. In fact, Bryan had been telling everyone in town that he had spent the last seven weeks writing his closing argument. He promised it would be the best speech he ever made.

✳  ✳  ✳  ✳

That morning, the crowds packed the courtroom and the heat was unbearable. A rumor began to circulate that the floor of the courthouse was in danger of collapsing because of the weight of all of the spectators. Judge Raulston ruled that the trial would be moved outside to the lawn. Scaffolding was quickly assembled to make a stage, and everyone rushed outside to find a good spot to watch. People climbed trees and crowded around the area. Darrow and Bryan had

William Jennings Bryan cools himself in the sweltering Dayton courtroom with a fan bearing an advertisement from Robinson's drugstore, where the plan to bring about the Scopes trial was hatched.

their biggest audience yet—nearly three thousand people (almost double the population of Dayton) waited for what they believed would be the closing arguments.

What the people didn't realize was that Darrow had a plan. Instead of starting his closing argument, Darrow said that he would like to call one more witness to the stand. The crowd was confused by this—hadn't Judge Raulston ruled that his witnesses couldn't testify? Darrow said that he wanted to call a "Bible expert" to the stand—a surprise witness. To everyone's amazement, Darrow announced that his surprise witness was Bryan.

Darrow (standing, left) questions a seated Bryan (just right of center). Fearing that the courtroom floor would collapse from the weight of the spectators packed inside, the judge moved the trial outside for the cross-examination.

Clarence Darrow (standing, with arms crossed) questions Bryan during the defense's examination. Though most people thought Darrow got the best of their exchange, some thought he was needlessly cruel to Bryan.

The other prosecuting attorneys begged Bryan not to testify. They suspected that Darrow was laying a trap for Bryan. However, to the shock of the audience and to the dismay of the other prosecuting attorneys, Bryan agreed to be an expert witness. The debate between Darrow and Bryan was finally going to happen.

"Do you believe that everything in the Bible should be literally interpreted?" Darrow asked.

"I believe that everything in the Bible should be accepted as it is given there," Bryan answered.

Darrow began questioning Bryan in a rapid-fire manner, trying to throw Bryan off and get him to contradict himself. Both lawyers became increasingly frustrated and angry at one another. Darrow asked Bryan difficult questions about events in the Bible, hoping to get Bryan to admit that some things in the Bible should not be taken literally.

"When exactly was the earth created?" "How many days did it take?" 'How was Eve made from Adam's rib?" "Where did Cain's wife come from?" Darrow did not back down as he paced in front of Bryan, questioning him about Biblical details. Finally, Darrow got what he had been hoping for. When Darrow asked Bryan about the length of time that it took to create the world, Bryan admitted that he did not personally believe in a literal interpretation of the Biblical account.

However, Bryan added that he didn't think that the fundamentalists who did believe in a literal interpretation were wrong, necessarily. "I think that it would be just as easy for the kind of God we believe in to make the earth in six days as in six years or in 6,000,000 years or in 600,000,000 years. I do not think it important whether we believe in one or the other," said Bryan.

"Do you think those were literal days?" countered Darrow.

"My impression is that they were periods, but I would not attempt to argue against anybody who wanted to believe in literal days," answered Bryan.

**IN MEMORIAM**

In 1930, fundamentalist Christians founded a college in Dayton, Tennessee, in honor of William Jennings Bryan. The small private school, named Bryan College, hosts a re-enactment of the Scopes trial every year. The school motto is "Christ Above All."

34

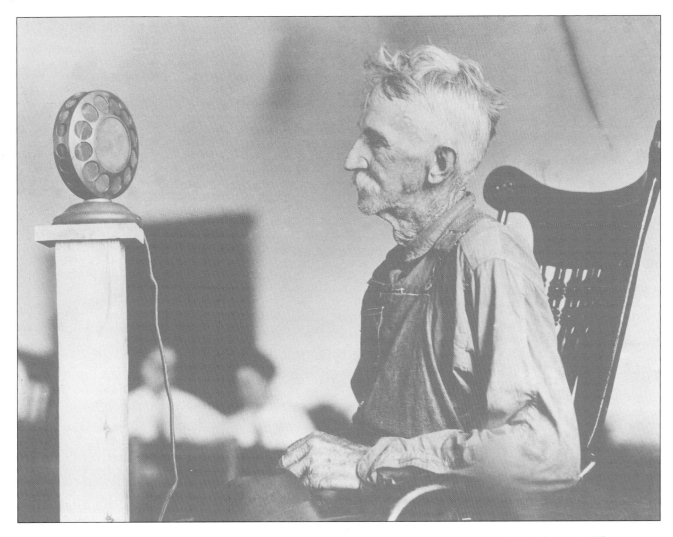

A local man testifies as a witness at the Scopes trial. He is speaking into a radio microphone; the Scopes case was the first trial to be broadcast nationwide.

It was not a total victory for Darrow, but many people who read about the exchange in the papers and heard the trial over the radio were quick to declare Darrow to be the winner of the debate. He had managed to get the most famous fundamentalist speaker in the country to admit that he did not personally believe in the literal interpretation of the

**Eleven of the twelve Scopes jurors were regular churchgoers. Ten were farmers from the countryside around Dayton.**

Biblical account of creation. The press reported on the event as though Bryan had been thoroughly defeated.

Many fundamentalists did not agree with this, however. They believed that Bryan's statement didn't prove anything, since Bryan had said that he wasn't sure if the Genesis account should be taken literally. Furthermore, many fundamentalists thought that Darrow was overly cruel when he questioned Bryan. Eloise Reed, who was 14 years old when she watched the trial, later told a reporter what she thought at the time:

"I sat right there in front of a platform where Clarence Darrow called William Jennings Bryan as his witness. From my point of view, Darrow made a monkey out of himself. Bryan

# STEINWAY TUNNEL OPENED TO TRAFFIC

## NEW YORK JOURNAL

FINAL NIGHT EXTRA

FINAL NIGHT EXTRA

# MONKEY TRIAL LAWYERS FIGHT OVER PRAYER OPENING COURT

### Thrill-Slayer Traced to Syracuse

**Six Chief Figures in Evolution Case**

These are the men whose activity has put the town of Dayton "on the map."

## DARROW OBJECTS TO "TURNING COURT INTO A MEETING HOUSE"

The Scopes trial was national news, as this headline from the *New York Journal* shows. The *Journal's* coverage was more tolerant than that of its rival paper, the *New York Times*, which reported that "half-wits" were "descending" on Dayton in support of the fundamentalists.

With the blistering summer heat making any activity seem unthinkable, idlers use the opportunity of the Scopes trial to do some constructive loitering on Market Street in Dayton.

held on to his belief in the Bible. They said sassy things to one another. I would have liked to have gotten up there and kicked Darrow because I thought he was being so unfair."

The debate ended the trial. Darrow had succeeding in getting a chance to debate Bryan. He decided that there was no point in continuing the trial after that point. To the shock and dismay of Bryan, Darrow announced that he wasn't going to make a closing statement. However, if the defense lawyer in a trial doesn't make a closing statement, it means that the prosecution is not allowed to make one either. Bryan was not allowed to give the closing speech that he had spent seven weeks writing. Instead, the verdict was quickly given. Scopes was found guilty and the judge fined him $100. A representative from a Baltimore newspaper paid Scopes' fine for him and he was set free. The trial of the century was over.

## THE AFTERMATH OF THE TRIAL

In the long run, Darrow and the ACLU never achieved their ultimate goal. Scopes' trial was indeed appealed to the Tennessee Supreme Court, but the court never ruled on whether or not the Butler Act was constitutional, as the ACLU hoped it they would. Instead, the Supreme Court pointed out that the jury was supposed to have set the amount of Scopes' fine, not Judge Raulston. This allowed the Supreme Court to dismiss the case. The court did rule that no one could ever be arrested under the law again, however. The Butler Act stayed on the books of Tennessee law until 1967, when the Tennessee legislature finally repealed it.

Today, evolution is taught in almost all of the public schools in America. The debate between the creationists and the evolutionists has never completely gone away, however.

In 1968, the U.S. Supreme Court ruled that evolution should be taught in public schools because it is based on science, but creationism cannot be taught in public schools, because it is based on religion.

In 1987, Louisiana tried to pass a law that said that creationism should be taught equally with evolution, but the Supreme Court once again ruled that teaching creationism violated the separation of church and state.

In 1999, the state of Kansas voted to remove all of the questions about evolution from their standardized tests. Many people objected to this, saying that it gave teachers an excuse to not teach evolution in class because the topic would never be tested. In 2001, the state returned the evolution questions to the tests.

Both Kansas and Alabama have also recently tried to pass laws saying that their state-approved biology textbooks must contain a statement that says that evolution is just a theory, not a proven fact.

In 2002, a town in Colorado also tried to pass a law allowing creationism to be taught equally in schools. The city government did not pass the law, however.

As you can see, the issue that first appeared in the tiny Tennessee town of Dayton is still being fought today in courtrooms across the country. On that hot July day in Dayton, a nation listened as an argument began over what we, as Americans, should teach our children in school. And America has been arguing about it ever since.

Fred Robinson, owner of the local drug store, poses with human and simian friends at the table in his store where Rappalyea, Scopes, and others planned the trial. Some of the planners acted out of genuine opposition to religious fundamentalism, while others saw the trial as a way to generate publicity that might save their dying town.

# Glossary

**agnostic**—a person who does not commit to believing in God

**conservative**—to believe in existing views and institutions and not sway from them; traditional

**constable**—a public officer of a town who is responsible for keeping the peace and minor judicial duties

**defendant**—a person who is required to answer for a legal action or suit that has been brought against him or her

**divine**—related to or originating from God or a god

**legislature**—a political unit of persons with the power to make laws

**liberal**—to not be strict or bound to tradition

**modest**—to hold a moderate view of one's self or abilities; to not be bold or assertive

**primates**—an order of mammals that includes humans, apes, and monkeys

**prosecution**—the party who is pursuing criminal charges against an offender in a court of law

**radicals**—people whose beliefs or practices are an extreme departure from what most of society considers traditional or normal beliefs and behavior

**rural**—country life or people; agricultural

**testify**—to make a statement based on personal knowledge or belief

**unconstitutional**—not consistent with the Constitution and, therefore, illegal

**vein**—a bed of useful mineral matter found in the earth

# Timeline: The Scopes

## 1859

Charles Darwin publishes *Origin of Species*, the first major text describing "evolution."

## 1913

The Cumberland Coal and Iron Company in Dayton declares bankruptcy, causing hundreds to lose their jobs.

## 1914

Hunter's Civic Biology is first published. Tennessee approves this book as their state biology text, and it is the text used by Dayton schools in 1925.

## 1918

World War **I** ends and American troops return from Europe.

## 1921

William Jennings Bryan retires from politics and begins his anti-evolution crusade.

## 1925

**MARCH 21**
Tennessee governor Austin Peay signs the Butler Act.

## 1987

Louisiana public schools attempt to teach creationism, but the U.S. Supreme Court rules against them

## 1999

Kansas removes evolution from standardized tests

## 2001

Kansas returns evolution to their standardized tests

## 2002

A town in Colorado briefly attempts to add creationism to the public school curriculum

# Trial

**MAY 4**
Newspapers in Tennessee carry an ad from the ACLU asking for volunteers to challenge the Butler Act.

**MAY 5**
George Rappalyea asks John Scopes to be the defendant in a test case of the Butler Act. Scopes agrees.

**JULY 10**
A jury for the Scopes Trial is picked.

**JULY 13**
Scopes Trial begins. Darrow asks Judge Raulston to "quash" the Butler Act—Raulston refuses.

**JULY 14**
Bryan presents the case for the prosecution.

**JULY 16**
Darrow's scientific witness testifies for

Judge Raulston, without the jury present.

**JULY 17**
Judge Raulston decides that Darrow's witnesses cannot testify before the jury. Darrow is charged with contempt, but Raulston drops the charge after Darrow apologizes.

**JULY 20**
The trial is moved to the lawn, and

Darrow calls Bryan as a witness. The debate lasts for 4 hours.

**JULY 21**
Darrow waives his closing arguments and asks for the verdict. After nine minutes of deliberation, the jury pronounces Scopes "guilty."

**JULY 26**
William Jennings Bryan dies in his sleep.

Bryan College, named after William Jennings Bryan, is founded in Dayton.

Clarence Darrow dies in Chicago. Tennessee repeals the Butler Act.

U.S. Supreme Court rules that evolution can be taught in public schools, but creationism cannot be taught.

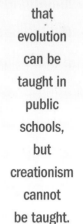

# To Find Out More

## BOOKS

Caudill, Edward, Edward J. Larson and Jesse Fox Mayshark. *The Scopes Trial: A Photographic History*. Knoxville, TN: U of Tennessee Press, 2000.

Hansen, Ellen. *Evolution on Trial*. Carlisle, MA: Discovery Enterprises Ltd., 1994.

Hanson, Freya Ottem. *The Scopes Monkey Trial: A Headline Court Case*. Berkeley Heights, NJ: Enslow, 2000.

## ONLINE SITES

American Experience: The Monkey Trial
*http://www.pbs.org/wgbh/amex/monkeytrial/*

Tennessee vs. John Scopes
*http://www.law.umkc.edu/faculty/projects/ftrials/scopes/scopes.htm*

Greatest Trials of All Time: The Scopes Monkey Trial
*http://courttv-web3.courttv.com/archive/greatesttrials/scopes/versus.html*

# Index

Bold numbers indicate illustrations.

# About the Author

**Renee Graves** is a freelance writer who lives in Memphis, Tennessee. She has a background in journalism and has worked for newspapers in Texas and Mississippi. She has also worked as a middle and high school English teacher, and most recently taught creative writing part-time at a local university. This is her first book for young people.